D1449014

Living in the Light of the Lord's Return

BIBLICAL HERITAGE SERIES No. 6

FELLOWSHIP OF CONCERNED MENNONITES
Harrisonburg, Virginia 22801

Biblical Heritage Series No. 6

Table of Contents

Table of Contents

Introduction

The messages contained in this booklet were delivered at the annual Bible Conference sponsored by the Fellowship of Concerned Mennonites, October 4-6, 1991 at the Plain View Church near Hutchinson, Kansas.

The theme of that conference was: Living in the Light of the Lord's Return (Heb. 10:25).

This is No. 6 in the Biblical Heritage Series produced by the Fellowship of Concerned Mennonites. The first was "Biblical Inerrancy and Reliability" by J. Otis Yoder and Harold S. Martin. The second pamphlet was on "Views of Salvation and How to Be Saved" by J. Ward Shank. The third in the series was "Biblical Perspectives on Women in Ministry" by Sanford C. Shetler. The fourth in the series was "Sanctity of Human Life and Biomedical Decision-making" by Paul E. Hooley, M.D. The fifth was "Vow Keepers–Vow Breakers" by Simon Schrock.

All six of these booklets are available at the special price of $12.00 Single copies are available for $2.95.

ONE

Living Expectantly

by Walter Beachy

THE TEXT IN I JOHN 3:1-3 stands out as one of the loftiest "I am" passages in all of Scripture about God's intent for His people. I would compare it favorably with II Peter 1 as well, where God's intention for His people in redemption comes through so clearly. Before we go to the passage, allow me to make several basic premises in relation to our expectations. First, I personally have a growing burden for the lack of spiritual fervor in the church. I am keenly aware that our lives are busier than they once were since we are not as dominantly agrarian-living and working on farms. Our young people's schedules are not as free as they once were, either. Many people under thirty on our church rolls as members quite often are missing in services. At least, they are not there regularly. The majority of people attending are older. There's a certain wistfulness among older people, longing for the way it used to be. We tend not to remember the negatives, only the positives, in the good old days. Someone said, "Note what's happening today, for twenty years down the road these shall be the good old days." That's a good idea, I suppose, but the fact remains that spiritual fervor is lacking. We have so many distractions, not only for the young, but for the old. One would have thought it never could happen, but we have older "couch potatoes" in the Mennonite Church. And I hope you don't even know what couch potatoes are. They are usually glued to a one-eyed monster much of the day and night.

A Lack of Fervor for the Things of the Lord. Why?

In our congregation, some may say, "Oh, Brother Dan is preaching," and their spirits soar because his way of preaching is different from mine. When I am scheduled to preach, their spirits will also soar or sag. You're all sitting there while I'm in an elevated position here behind a pulpit. We are trained to think in terms of responding to what's happening up front. You become an audience and I, the preacher, become a performer. I accept the awesome responsibility of preaching, but where is God in the audience/performer equation? Is it any wonder He can break into a service where people are focused in that direction? I think it should be a test of ordination qualifications that a preacher will not refer to the congregation as an audience. Now that's a hyperbole! But I think it's really serious. We ought to change that. When we get to the house of the Lord, when we go into our closets, when we meditate during the day, we ought to expect to meet God! If we operate from that basis, then fervor will not be lacking—or at least the fuel for fervor.

The Importance of Expectation

Have you ever considered how often you act out of your expectations? Think how much your actions are affected by what you expect. I don't really expect, as I'm speaking, to hear many "amens". I would be delighted to be surprised and proven wrong. We act out of our expectations. If we really expect the Lord to break through the clouds one day and come to the earth as lightning, and, as

Paul describes it, "in a moment, in the twinkling of an eye" we'll be changed. If we really expect that, won't that affect our lives? Won't that affect our churches? I think so. We act out of our expectations and our expectations affect us emotionally. Sometimes when expectations are very flat and almost nonexistent or negative, our emotions are negative, sad or just flat. But if our expectations are high, then we have different emotions.

Recently we were at a wedding in Canada. That young groom was absolutely charged with expectation! So was the bride! Both of them were somewhat quiet, but in their own quiet ways literally glowed. A little different from some marriage situations with which I've been involved. But expectations at the marriage altar are so often quite different from what really happens after the wedding.

We cannot begin to imagine what God is going to do for us and to us. The apostle Paul says, "Eye hasn't seen, ear hasn't heard, neither has entered into the heart of man what God has prepared for them that love Him." Paul is talking about us right now. In this age. In the Old Testament, prophets desired to look into the many things they prophesied and couldn't understand. Peter writes about the gospel being such that angels desired to look into the things they were involved in as ministering spirits. And we go to sleep hearing it preached! We get bored after years of experiencing it! You see the problem? I wonder how many times our guardian angels wonder what's going on. After all that it cost the Lord and all He's done and plans yet to do! Our expectations tell us something very significant about the spiritual dynamics going on in our minds and hearts.

I would suppose that most of us would have to admit that our spiritual expectations reflect our spiritual lives. Does fervor create expectation or does expectation create fervor? Can one even separate fervor and expectation? Our expectations are basically created and focused by three major things. One is information, another is our choice of desires and thirdly is faith. The Bible tells us to set our affections on things above and to delight ourselves in the law of the Lord. We choose what will delight us. I'm convinced that God who made us understands us better than any psychologist or psychiatrist. He told us to take charge of our delights and focus them where we ought. And if He told us that, we can do it! We can choose to feed one kind of delights or desires that are carnal, negative or temporal or we can choose to feed another kind of desires and delights that are spiritual and eternal. We are commanded to do the latter. So we obviously can do it. So it's *information, desires,* and *faith.* The Bible mentions the gift of faith. Saving faith is something we can either embrace or not. Saving faith is ours by choice, but the gift of faith is given by the Spirit. I believe we need to ask God for faith. But we also need to do the things that create faith in God. Unless we have information, desire and faith we will hardly have expectations.

Information comes several ways. Some information is intuitive. No one has to tell us; it's innate within us. There are four things we intuitively know. The first is that there is a God. Everyone intuitively knows that. For example, in Russia they taught the opposite of intuitive knowledge and it still didn't destroy the intuition. In fact, in the '50s they did a survey in Russia of high school students–57% of them believed that there is a God in spite of 12 years of atheistic indoctrination. So they decided to redouble their efforts and strengthen the curriculum in teaching atheism. Ten years later they did another survey and belief in God was up ten points! It didn't work because the officials were bucking something that is intuitive, God-placed. I've never seen adult birds trying to teach young birds to build nests. They just intuitively know how. Baltimore orioles will build hanging nests without ever being told or shown how to do it–they just do it. Only God could put that in them! The little hummingbirds that fly and feed around our place will tank up some day and head south. They will go as far south of the equator as they are north now, flying up to 80 miles an hour. They know exactly where they are going. Those that survive the season are very apt to wind up back at our place. We frequently lose our way even with maps! Hummingbirds don't have maps! They just fly it.

We intuitively know there's a God. We also intuitively know what is right and wrong. We have moral consciousness. We might not always have it right–but we are quite consistent with the ten commandments. Paul spoke of that when he said that those who naturally do the things contained in the law show that it is written in their hearts. Who put it there? God did. So we have intuitive moral information and, consequently, we also have guilt because we have all sinned. Thus we have an intuitive religious sense. Everyone has some kind of religion, even if it's atheism. Fourthly, everybody has a sense of immortality. We're going to live on somewhere beyond this life. It's intuitive.

We as Christians also have a lot of objective information that, hopefully, becomes subjective–that is, the Bible. It stands outside and above us. We hear its words and absorb its ideas and its truths, and then they become subjective to us. Even if we reject them or are ignorant of them, they still stand. Whatever we do with the Bible doesn't change its truth. As Christians, we need to embrace the truth as revealed in the Scriptures.

Christian faith has an evidential and rational basis. After 41 years as a Christian, I have never yet run across anything that God expects me to believe that is contrary to reason. Think about that a bit. I've been asked to believe things that didn't immediately make sense or cannot be explained or ever expected scientifically. We live in an open system where God is both above this cosmos and in it. He who created the laws of which our scientists are aware, also can step into this cosmos and do anything He chooses to do. That's a very rational thing to believe–in line with my own intuitive knowledge. So, consequently, miracles are not irrational, they are supernatural. My expectations reflect to a large extent how I've been thinking, desiring and informing my mind. When I respond either in belief or disbelief, then my expectations follow.

I don't know how John would have preached from I John 3:1-3. He was an old man when he wrote those words. I can hear him say, "look, gaze upon, behold, what manner of love the Father has bestowed upon us, that we should be called. . . ." *We,* that's a loaded personal pronoun. Who are you? Do you deserve it? We should be called the sons of God. Then he says, "Therefore the world doesn't know us–didn't know him." We're called the sons of God because we're the sons of God while the majority out there are not. Then he says, "Beloved, *now* are we the sons of God and it doesn't yet appear what we shall be, but we know that when HE appears, we shall be like him." The Greek would be even more obvious, I'm told, than the English–*for* or *because* we will see Him like He is. Then this is a natural consequence, "every man that has this hope in him will purify himself even as He is pure." We have this hope in Jesus. We have expectations in Jesus and they reside in our minds, in our spirits. We don't really have any hope unless it's in Jesus and if we have this hope we have something exciting happening inside of us that resides in our spirit. We have this hope in Him.

If we do, we will purify ourselves; we purify what we think; purify what we read; we purify our mediations; we purify our desires; we purify our moral character. The spirit of God is in us and the word of God is in our minds and our hope is in the Lord.

Based on what He already has done, we have the basis and the spiritual power in Jesus to become essentially and substantially what God wants us to become in this life and in the life to come. In this life and the next, most of what happens to us as Christians happens because of our expectations. Now, probably that's truer in this life than in the next, but if you apply it specifically to this life there is no end to its applications.

If you are born with particular family traits, what are your expectations of what God can do? I'm a Beachy so I'm going to have to be a servant of my stubbornness and temper!! Is that right? NO! We underestimate what God wants to do NOW. I know my message is to focus on the future and living expectantly in light of the Lord's return, but I believe that we will not really expect very much there until we have know the joy, the thrill of being changed NOW. We have a downpayment and we have an actual experience of what God can do. I can't say enough of what God has done for my temper. He didn't take all of the backbone out of me, but He gave me grace not to be as unkind to my wife as I have been at times. I won't bore you with those details and embarrass myself, but I know there's grace. I also know the thrill of loving people who are hard to love in the flesh. I say all of this to be praise of God's grace! Look at that grace. From this passage I would point out two things—first. the word *behold*. The idea is to think about it; to look at it; to gaze upon it. What has God been doing in your life and what does He want to do?

The determinists say that all we are and all that we do

issues from our genes, environment, or our body chemistry. All those are important factors. I do not deny my genetic corruption and its influence upon me. I do not deny that my environment affects me. My body chemistry affects me. But where in the equation is the grace of God? Where is the free will of man to make choices? Behold what God has done! Gaze upon the love of God and then "we will be like him when he comes" because we see Him as He is. There is a divine principle that our focus upon the Lord will be the means of our change. When we actually see the glorified Jesus we'll be made like Him! The principle works now! Paul says, "We all with unveiled face looking upon the glory of the Lord are changed into the same image from glory to glory even as by the spirit of the Lord."

There's a basic principle in Scripture that without faith it's impossible to please God. A practical rule of thumb is that our expectations are born of our faith. Faith comes from information. As a Christian, you will hardly ever experience that for which you have no faith. Think about that. Sometimes God throws us a pleasant surprise but almost always what we experience issues out of what we have some information about and have embraced in belief.

Now, back to our passage. Look at the love of God and what He's doing now. "Now are we the sons of God." Have we experienced and are we experiencing evidences of sonship? Made in His image. Do we have the hope that will allow us to live expectantly in this era of apostasy and also of harvest?

It's a strange mix going on today. I think we should pray for revival and hope for it to happen. Plead with God to let it happen before Jesus comes.

Some day we'll look upon the face of Jesus and never die again. Praise God, He's going to make us like Himself. He appeared to John on the Isle of Patmos and said, "I am he that was dead but, behold, I'm alive forevermore. And I have the keys of death and the grave." Praise God, He has the keys and not the devil! He's got the keys of the grave and death! We don't have to fear death because He's going to let us out. In fact, He went one step beyond that. He said, "He that believes in me though he were dead, yet shall he live." We'll never die! Let's translate that into the experience of our churches. What do you believe about your brother or sister whose besetting sin is obvious? Do you believe God can change it? What do you believe about your neighbor or son or daughter? Do you believe God could change them?

Every church, every person needs to see persons changed who once were in the depths of sin and now are totally new creatures! Praise God for His grace by which we can live expectantly in this life facing the future with great anticipation!

Walter Beachy is the Chairman of FCM; leader in the Conservative Mennonite Church and of the United Bethel Congregation, Plain City, OH.

TWO

How Shall We Live Reverently?

by Simon Schrock

SMILE, GOD LOVES YOU! That's the message we see on bumper stickers, T-shirts, pins, cards and coffee cups. We have been saying it for years to the unsaved and to Christians in distress. And it's true–God loves you!

While having lunch in a restaurant, I noticed an untidy person smoking a cigarette and wearing a T-shirt with this message: "Yes, Jesus loves you."

Jesus does love you! But tell me: Why are believers so reckless in their behavior? Why so casual and irreverent in their conduct? Why so easily drawn into the world's entertainment? Why such lack of respect and dignity in God's house of worship? How can we profess to "seek first the kingdom of God," but first pursue our own interests? Why do believers go against their better knowledge of Scripture? How can believers pad their pockets and hoard wealth, then just "tip" God while the work of the Church suffers? How can a Christian woman believe I Corinthians II, I Peter 3, and follow fashionable fads? How is it that someone can make a vow before God to be faithful to a marriage partner until death, break that vow, then marry another person? How can practicing homosexuals claim "God's love" and ridicule church leaders for not receiving them into the church fellowship? Why can a Christian student on a "Christian college" campus dress in beach wear and listen to rock music that sounds like a midnight casino? How can people twist and turn the Word of God to make it say what they want?

Could it be there is a dimension of God and discipleship that is being overlooked? Have believers lost or overlooked something? I think so!

Have you ever noticed how children take advantage of a parent that is too loving to say NO? A child soon catches on when there is no restraint. Many adults are merely grown children. We continue behavior in much the same way–except with a better mask.

We have been told over and over again, "Smile, God loves you!" It is repeated to persons practicing and planning sin. And it's true–God loves you!

On the other hand, there is subconsciously an undercurrent of thought that has many believing that God loves us–and only winks at our sins.

Yes, there is a missing dimension in the way many view God. That missing dimension is this–*God is holy.* There ought to be a matching bumper sticker to place beside "Smile, God Loves You." I propose this–*"Have Reverence for God–He Is Holy."*

Could it be that believers are cultivating a lopsided view of God? I think so! We are very much like children; the heavenly Father will overlook it. He is loving; He loves me. Grace abounds!

Therefore, what was once sin, is now condoned. Others do it, and judgment didn't come, so it must not be so bad. False doctrine is accepted. Half-truth is taught and a partial Gospel becomes the accepted norm.

A person's view of God affects behavior. If I only know John 3:16, the love side of God, then I will likely have faulty behavior. The Bible calls that "lukewarm."

Jesus said:

> Not every one that saith unto me, Lord, Lord, shall enter
> into the kingdom of heaven; but he that doeth the will of
> my Father which is in heaven.

> Many will say to me in that day, Lord, Lord, have we not
> prophesied in thy name? and in thy name have cast out
> devils? and in thy name done many wonderful works?

> And then will I profess unto them, I never knew you: depart
> from me, ye that work iniquity.   –Matthew 7:21-23

Many in the church have lost the wonder and meaning of this teaching.

Many prefer just to say, "Smile, God loves you." However, if we can understand and grasp that "not every one
that sayeth . . . Lord . . . shall enter the kingdom of heaven,
but *he that doeth the will of my Father which is in heaven,*"
and if we can understand that *God is holy,* it will make a
difference in our behavior. Persons who realize that *God
is holy* will be careful how they live. Only those who do
the will of the Father shall enter the kingdom.

If a man sees only a loving God who winks at sin,
then he may go to church, sing the church hymns, say
"praise God," and repeat prayers. He may shake hands
with the preacher and say, "Fine sermon, Reverend." Now
that he has done his Sunday morning duty, he may stop at
Shoney's on the way home, stuff himself from the salad
bar, go on home, change into "cut-offs" and mow the grass.
In the meanwhile, his twelve-year-old daughter may be
curled in the recliner, being entertained by the "tube," and
his wife may run down the street to take advantage of a
Sunday evening special.

Yes–God loves you. It's true that grace abounds.
However, the Bible says:

> What shall we say then? Shall we continue in sin that grace
> may abound?

> God forbid. How shall we, that are dead to sin, live any
> longer therein?
>
> Knowing this, that our old man is crucified with him, that
> the body of sin might be destroyed, that henceforth we
> should not serve sin.   –Romans 6:1, 2, 6

I am convinced that much of the behavior we see in
the church today is mockery and blasphemy against God.
It does not show reverence or respect for His holiness.
"Holy" is used more often as a prefix to His name than any
other attribute.

> And the Lord spake unto Moses, saying, Speak unto all the
> congregation of the children of Israel and say unto them,
> Ye shall be holy: for I the Lord your God am holy.
>   –Leviticus 19:1-2
>
> Exalt the Lord our God, and worship at His holy hill, for
> the Lord our God is holy.   –Psalm 99:9

Isaiah got a glimpse of God's holiness and wrote about
what he saw:

> In the year that King Uzziah died, I saw also the Lord sitting
> upon a throne, high and lifted up, and His train filled the
> temple.
>
> About it stood the seraphim: each one had six wings; with
> twain he covered his face, and with twain he covered his
> feet , and with twain he did fly.
>
> And one cried to another, and said, Holy, holy, holy, is the
> Lord of hosts: the whole earth is full of His glory.
>   -Isaiah 6:1-3

"Holy, holy, holy, is the Lord of hosts." This attribute
of God is being overlooked. The holiness of God is mentioned in Scripture before His love, and more often. To
really be able to comprehend God's love, and smile, one
must understand something of His holiness.

What does *holy* mean in reference to God? Why is it so important? It means that God is morally blameless. He always does what is just and right. Holiness is one of God's attributes and part of His very nature.

This means: "God is light, and in Him is no darkness at all" (I John 1:5). He cannot look on wickedness with favor. He cannot overlook any sin we commit. As the Bible says: "Your eyes are too pure to look on evil, you cannot tolerate wrong" (Habakkuk 1:13, NIV).

Because He is holy, He hates sin (Zechariah 8:17). Because He is holy, He cannot accept excuses. (He does accept repentance and confession.)

When we sin, we do something God hates. He hates pride, jealousy, selfishness, lustful thoughts, lukewarm commitments, outbursts of anger and our reasoning that the end justifies sinful means. While we become so accustomed to our sins, we can live in peaceful co-existence with them; God never ceases to hate them. Your sins and wrong attitudes toward your brothers and sisters are sins against God.

Because of His holiness, He hates sin wherever it is found. He does not overlook sin. He does not hate one person's sin and overlook it in another. That is against His very nature.

As the Scripture says: "The Father, who without respect of persons, judgeth according to every man's work" (I Peter 1: 17).

God is sinless. He cannot sin. How does the realization of this affect our behavior? Take a person who swears and uses foul language. If you let him know you do not appreciate it, the reply may be, "Sorry about that. I didn't know you are a 'Reverend.' " That is the way we humans are; we behave better in front of "holy people" than we do before a Holy God!

Engraved on a tombstone of a dear little girl were these

words: "It was easier to be good when she was with us."

Lord Peterborough said about Fenelon: "I was forced to get away from him, else he would have made me pious."

Just as it is easier to behave better around holy people, it is easier to live godly when you realize God is holy. May God's holiness move us to piety!

Am I downplaying the love of God? No! This is a call for balance. Balance is like a stereo. You hear love and holiness in balance. Each is giving its clear message. The message is: *Smile, God loves you,* and *Reverence God, He is holy.*

How shall we live reverently?

1. Make sure of your holy position in Christ. We must see sin as being against God. Evil attitudes, selfishness, stubbornness, pride, lust of the flesh are sins against God. These traits are not just personal defects or treatable illnesses, but sins against God. Much of our grieving is over our reputation and what it does to us, instead of grieving over displeasing a holy God. King David expressed a godly sorrow over his sin of adultery when he said, "I have sinned against the Lord" (II Samuel 12:13). The prodigal son returned to his father and said, "I have sinned against heaven" (Luke 15:21).

I, like David and the prodigal son, have sinned against God. I need the salvation of Jesus Christ. Because of what Jesus Christ has done for me at Calvary, I can be released from the judgment of sin and be set free. Be sure you have by faith trusted Jesus Christ to forgive you all your sins and sinfulness. Be sure you have come to Jesus with a broken spirit, like David and sought God's forgiveness. When that has happened, you can claim forgiveness, and have a righteous position before God.

2. Pursue holiness as a way of life. Since you have been forgiven and now have a holy position before God,

His Word calls you to live a holy life. The Bible calls believers to be holy, walk in holiness, follow peace and holiness and become more like Christ.

> According as he hath chosen us be holy and without blame before him in love. —Ephesians 1:4

> Let every one of you that nameth the name of Christ depart from iniquity. —II Timothy 2:19

Holiness is required for our ongoing fellowship with God, and assurance of salvation. The only safe evidence that we are in Christ is a holy life. Holiness is necessary, too, for effective service to God.

3. Reject the comparison method.

> But they, measuring themselves by themselves, and comparing themselves among themselves, are not wise. —II Corinthians 10:12b

How can believers say, "Smile, God loves you," and do some of the things they do? Because they live by the comparison method rather than the Word of God.

They reason: Bob is a professional football player who plays on Sundays. He is a Christian, so it must be all right. Mary is a Christian; she prays and witnesses. She has short hair and doesn't wear a veiling, so it must not be that important. Some military people are good Christians; why not take them into the church? Baptized infants express faith, so why not receive them? "Gay believers" claim the love of God; why can't they be members? The list could go on and on. The idea is that if God hasn't zapped them with judgment, the behavior must be acceptable.

The comparison method hinders holy living. It pulls us down by building on weakness.

4. Beware of the "Cultural Boundary." To a degree, the legal system allows a community to decide what is ac-

ceptable reading material at the local drugstore. If the community deems it pornographic, it can be kept out. That is an adjustable standard according to the community.

The Lord does not change his standards of holiness. Even so, believers still tend to allow the culture to dictate what is acceptable behavior. We become accustomed to our environment and consider it to be the "norm." We need to remember God never accepted Israel's idol worship or blending into the pagan culture. Has God accepted a culture that goes against His Word?

The challenge for believers is to reject ungodly culture. Culture boundaries are not a safe guide to living reverently in light of Christ's return.

5. Live by the Book. How do we face the issues around us? We are constantly being introduced to new issues–AIDS, safe sex, abortion, and suicide. What's the answer?

When I had my first Ford, I would go to the local garage and inquire about parts. A familiar expression was, "I'll have to look it up in the book."

How shall we live in this adulterous and sinful generation? Look it up in the Book–the Word of God. Examine everything under the light of the Word of God.

> For God hath not called us unto uncleanness, but unto holiness.   –I Thessalonians 4:7

Yes, smile, God loves you! But do not forget to respect Him, because he is holy!

Simon Schrock is the leader in the Beachy Amish Church at Catlett, Virginia. This message was given at the 1991 FCM Annual Bible Conference in Kansas.

THREE

Living Obediently in the Light of the Lord's Return

by Henry Plank

THE GENERAL THEME of this Bible conference is indeed an exciting one. Nothing is more thrilling than the anticipation of the imminent return of our Lord. As we approach the end of this century, we can expect the false prophets to appear. We would do well to be aware of that; watch and pray that we not be moved by them.

Obedience does not rate high on the popularity chart of today's sermons. What is popular among men may not impress our Lord. It is sad that preachers sometimes get on the popularity bandwagon. Unpopular sermons may be the most needed. We have all kinds of seminars on church growth, marriage and how to get along with ourselves and others, but no seminars on obedience.

Why So Little About Obedience?

Why do we hear so little about obedience when the Scripture emphasizes it? I offer a few observations for our consideration. I believe a world-view dominates every culture. To properly understand what is happening within that culture, it is important that we understand what that world-view is.

It is fascinating to observe how these world-views

change in times of crisis. It is also interesting to see how these world-views permeate everything within a culture, including theology itself. The preacher should be aware of the world-view that dominates the culture in which he lives lest his sermons simply become a product of that view.

Francis Shaeffer in his book, *The Church at the End of the 20th Century,* mentions the "Silent Majority." They like the old ways but may never stop to realize why they do the things they do. They like the comfortable ways of life; they go to work; they have their children, but seldom bother to look at the larger picture of what makes our society the way it is. He maintains that this group of people is the greatest liability the church has. Add the modern media with television to the list of influences in their lives and you have a "Silent Majority" that lives with a rusty brain refusing to think. This is a tragedy in both church and society.

How does all this fit into the picture of what has happened in relation to obedience? There is always good and bad in any world-view. I will point out the defects and how they affect us.

What Has Happened?

There was a movement of thought that began in the latter part of the 18th century and continued through the 19th century into the 20th century, called the Enlightenment. The slogan of this movement was–"Have the courage to make use of your understanding." It was also called the Age of Reason. Men thought they could find truth through absolute reason. The good side of this was the birth of modern science. The bad side was that this was applied to the Scriptures. Reason has some definite limitations. The miracles in the Bible cannot be explained by human reason. So the miracles of the Bible were denied.

The virgin birth was denied as well as the inspiration of the Scriptures. Man was now at the helm and it was up to him to decide what was and was not true in the Bible.

Liberal thought reached a crisis about 1917 during World War I. The ugliness of war revealed that man was evil in his heart. Some theologians such as Karl Barth went back to the Scripture for the answers but still retained much liberal theology. They introduced what has been called neo-orthodoxy, a new kind of orthodoxy. How do you arrive at truth from a Bible that contains errors as these theologians taught? The answer was that you find it within yourself. Existentialism, which means that reality is determined by experience, became the prevailing world-view of this new theology, which held that the Bible becomes the Word of God because of the way one experiences it. Many thought this was a return to orthodox theology, but it was not. Truth must be experienced but it does not arise out of personal experience. The charismatic movement is related to this world-view. The emphasis was on gifts, instead of fruit, and obedience was not emphasized.

This truth-by-experience route went to seed about 1980 in what is called the New Age Movement. This movement is not new but is the second oldest religion in the world, the one Satan introduced to Eve when he promised her she would be god if she obeyed him. When she obeyed Satan, she disobeyed God. It is still that way today. Ever since that time, Satan has been promoting a religion in which man can be his own God. We could call this religious humanism. Man plays the part of God in false religious systems.

Through the influence of this truth-by-experience kind of theology and secular psychology, both of which deny the actuality of the fall of man as a historical event, we have the New Age Movement. This New Age philosophy is affecting what is being taught and practiced in our Mennonite and Amish churches In my years of preaching, I have seen a drastic change in what is coming across the pulpit. Many sermons are baptized secular psychology in which we are told that man's basic problem is not sin, but a low self-esteem. He needs to find himself. He needs to feel good about himself. The idea behind this is that man is basically good. The Bible teaches that man is basically evil and needs salvation.

The Bible predicts that in the last days it will be difficult to be a Christian because of this self-religion. II Timothy teaches that perilous tinies shall come. Why? Because men shall be lovers of themselves. This self-religion makes what God says about man and his obligation to obey seem unimportant. The requirement Jesus gave for discipleship was to deny, not to love one's self. Self-denial never has been popular and it never will be. Self-denial, cross-bearing and suffering are requirements for following Jesus Christ.

Instead of urging repentance, confession, restitution and forgiveness, we send people off to a counselor. A good dose of obedience, repentance and restitution would solve many problems and make people feel much better about themselves.

I can still remember a few incidents from my childhood days in relationship to my father. I had a good father. I believe when he asked me to do something he had my best interest at heart. I didn't always feel the same as he did and at times I disobeyed. I also remember the emotional distress I felt when I disobeyed him. Physical distress at times also accompanied my disobedience! How good it felt when I obeyed and could see my father's smile at his obedient son! The same is true in my relationship to my heavenly father. When I obey him as his Word teaches,

I feel good about myself because I am pleasing him. Thus I enjoy the right kind of freedom.

My assignment is to discuss obedience in the light of the Lord's return and how it relates to missions. I have chosen to use the parable of the nobleman in Luke 19 as a basis for the message. In that parable, faithfulness is another word which is inseparable from obedience. Success is no substitute for faithfulness. We are not called to be successful, but faithful. Success is often the way the world looks at us, but faithfulness is what God sees. I believe that faithful people are also obedient people.

This parable is a proper illustration describing the relationship between obedience in the light of the Lord's return and missions. The parable is set in the context of missions. Preceding the parable, there is the well-known story of the conversion of the social outcast, Zaccheus. The murmuring Pharisees are there with their accusations— "This man is gone to be a guest with a man who is a sinner," they complain. The verse preceding the parable states, "For the Son of Man is come to seek and to save that which was lost." This is the reason Jesus came and it is still the mission of the church. The biggest problem among men is sin which has separated man from his God.

The purpose of the parable is clearly stated. First, because he was nigh to Jerusalem. What does that mean? He was making his final trip to Jerusalem where he was going to suffer and die. But they wanted a different Messiah who would throw off the Roman yoke. Church history tells us that. Satan has been busy with his false prophets carving out a different Jesus than the one in the Bible. This is not new. In II Pet. 2:1, we read, "But there were false prophets also among the people, even as there shall be false prophets among you who privily shall bring in damnable heresies, even denying the Lord that bought them, and bring upon themselves swift destruction."

These false prophets, which are numerous today, deny the virgin birth and the deity of Jesus Christ. If we are going to offer salvation to those who are lost, there must be a Saviour from sin. He must be one who is both God and man, Jesus Christ. Every generation seems to want to carve out its own Messiah. When we depart from the Scripture, we have a Christ of our own imagination which can never be a Saviour of mankind. The deity of Jesus Christ was the stumbling block for the Jews in Jesus' day and is also for the skeptics and unbelievers in our day.

The second reason he gave the parable was because they thought the kingdom of God should immediately appear. Some will not agree with me when I say that the kingdom of God and the church are not the same in Scripture. Jesus said to Peter, "Thou art Peter and upon this rock will I build (not my kingdom) my church." If they are the same, then we should be able to use the words interchangeably. One's theology and eschatology will make a difference in his view of the church, the kingdom and missions. The people who teach Dominion Theology are out to build the kingdom. We certainly are not going to bring in the kingdom by putting the proper political machinery in place.

The church is described as a mystery which was hid in other ages and is now made known. The apostle Paul made it clear that this mystery was made known to the apostles (Eph. 3:4-7). The church began on the day of Pentecost and it is not proper to speak of the church prior to Pentecost. The church did not begin until after the resurrection of Jesus Christ and the day of Pentecost.

In this parable, a nobleman, the king's son, went into a far country to receive for himself a kingdom. In this far country, in preparation for this kingdom, he called ten servants and gave each a pound. The king's son left and told his servants to occupy until his return. His citizens which hated him were the Jewish leaders who rejected him. The commission was given to his servants to do business until the king's son returns. Each is given a pound (about $20) to invest until he returns. After he returns, those who have been given the responsibility need to give account of their stewardship. The kingdom doesn't begin until after the nobleman returns. To me, this parable illustrates missions in the absence of the king's son. We are awaiting that return which we believe is imminent.

The Command–Occupy Till I Come

To occupy until the king's son returns simply means to do business for him. To invest that which has been entrusted to his servants while he is away is not a ridiculous nor unreasonable command. He is not asking them to be successful, but faithful. I know from experience that we can become very self-centered in mission work. Some are in it for what they can get out of it. It is sad when ministries are built around some charismatic person. Many have ministered in their own interest instead of the interest of the Lord Jesus Christ, and have failed.

He gave each steward a pound. There was no excuse for irresponsibility on the part of any. G. Campbell Morgan said the pound is the deposit of the gospel. I agree.

In this parable, Jesus was preparing his disciples for their work which began with the church at Pentecost. Jesus did this on other occasions, as in the mystery parables in Matthew 13 which he explained to his disciples.

The great commission is to go to all the world and make disciples. Some have mistaken the command and have gone to sheep-counting instead of making disciples. Adding numbers to the roll does not necessarily mean we are acting in the interest of the king's son or being faithful. The cults seem to add numbers faster than the faithful. How people are attracted by numbers and program!

The early church was illegal and persecuted, but they were on fire for God. Today we have become complacent and many times like the Laodicean church. We have become rich and lukewarm concerning our task in missions. We spend a lot of time trying to make the gospel presentable without any offense. The true gospel will always be an offense. It will upset people. The Jewish leaders were upset because the disciples spoke the word of God with boldness.

One such occasion is recorded in Acts 4:13 where we read, "Now when they saw the boldness of Peter and John and perceived that they were ignorant and unlearned men, they marveled; and they took knowledge of them, that they had been with Jesus." They took knowledge that they had been doing business for the king's son. Their life and testimony revealed they had been with Jesus. That, after all, is what the world is looking for. My prayer for myself in the ministry of our Lord is–Do I remind them of Jesus Christ?

Jesus said that when He, the Holy Spirit, is come, he will not speak of himself, but will glorify me. He does not glorify some church program or individual, but Jesus Christ. In his absence, the church is to occupy–do business until he returns.

The Compliments–
Well Done, Thou Good and Faithful Servant

Jesus never received many compliments. He did receive much opposition and criticism. His critics brought a sick person on the Sabbath day to see what he would do. Most of the things he did were not sanctioned by the religious leaders. They wanted to get rid of him because he challenged their programs.

When he went into the house of Zacchaeus, he was criticized for it.

Jesus warned us to be on guard when the world speaks well of us, when they extend their greetings of praise in the marketplace.

The compliment from the nobleman when he returned was, "Well done, thou good servant. . . ." Some gained more pounds than others. Let God take care of the arithmetic and let us take care of being faithful. He, no doubt, has a different set of books than ours. During the process of being faithful, the numbers came. That is a picture of the early church. The Lord did the adding and the church did the occupying–business for the king's son.

I would like to see some seminars on obedience and faithfulness. If we are faithful, we will declare the whole counsel of God. Faithful means to be full of faith. When we believe, we also obey. When we disobey, we don't believe and are unfaithful.

In the eyes of the world we may be successful. God puts the premium of faithfulness within the reach of all.

The Condemnation–Take It From Him

The time of reckoning will come when he will return and his servants will give an account of their stewardship of the gospel. He will deal with his servants and his enemies. This can be a joyous occasion if we are faithful, but a sad occasion if we are unfaithful. There is a varied response and each is dealt on the basis of his faithfulness in doing business for the king's son. The English language has no sweeter words than, "Well done, thou good and faithful servant," at the end of life.

The last steward was outright disobedient. He had no

interest in doing business for the king's son. Notice, he came saying, "Lord, behold, here is thy pound which I have kept laid up in a napkin." The Lord never told him to do that. It was his excuse. He didn't say, "I was too busy with my own schedule to do what you told me to do." He, no doubt, had salved his own conscience to his own satisfaction. In every church a committed group of people can be counted on to be faithful. Unfortunately, many churches also have the kind that can make excuses for their indifference and have done it so often they can lie without pangs of conscience. Matt. 7:21-23 says, "Not everyone that saith, 'Lord, Lord,' shall enter the kingdom of heaven, but he that doeth the will of my father which is in heaven."

This champion excuse-maker, instead of a confession of his laziness, lack of concern and spiritual indifference, plays the famous blame gave. It is all the preacher's fault. If the church were more spiritual. . . . It all started in the Garden of Eden when Adam blamed Eve and continues today. Someday, for all, reality will come when the King's son returns.

This type, a real trouble-maker in the church, may put on a good front but is bitter and faultfinding inside, and, most of all, he is bitter against God. His conscience bothers him because of his hypocrisy. There are no happy hypocrites.

The steward placed the blame on the ridiculous character of the nobleman and thought this would get him off the hook. This is often the way it works. People take their bitterness out on other people when they are having difficulties in their relationship with the Lord. But the bottom line is they are bitter toward God.

The nobleman could see right to the heart of the matter. It reveals how excuses will work in the day of reckoning for the Lord will judge in truth and righteousness.

The man knew and the Lord knew that this man was not interested in doing business for Him. He was a first-class hypocrite in what he was saying. He was in the church–a servant, yes, but an unfaithful one. His real problem was disobedience and he knew it. He could have at least put it in the bank. He was no better off than the Jews which hated him.

I think there is a lesson here for the church. The stewardship of the gospel was given to the Jewish people who were unfaithful. The pound was taken from the unfaithful servant and given to the one who was faithful. If we, as Mennonites, become unfaithful in our stewardship of the gospel, the pound will be taken from us and given to those who are faithful. We must concentrate on being faithful in our stewardship of the gospel. If we are not, we are no better than the Jewish nation was.

Henry Plank is bishop and pastor at North Vine St. Conservative Mennonite Church, Arthur, IL.

FOUR

The Nature of the Bible
Christ the Central Figure

by J. Otis Yoder

WE MUST DEFINE our terms before we begin our discussion of this topic. By *nature* we mean the essential quality. The Bible is the Book of books. It is unequaled in all the writings of all people of all time. It is unique for it is the revelation to man of the supreme God given by that God.

The word "Bible" has come to define the Christian assurance that those sixty-six books are much more than an anthology of assorted sacred writings of pious men purporting to speak for deity. Rather that collection of books constitutes the sum total of written revelation of the all-holy God to the whole human race. IT IS THE BOOK OF GOD. It is the BOOK FROM GOD not merely a book about God.

The Bible provides us with otherwise unattainable spiritual insights into the meaning of life and historical events. The meaning of the Exodus of the people of Israel from the bondage of Egypt goes far beyond the liberation of a pack of Hebrew slaves from their oppressors in the ancient world.

The formation of the tribes of Israel into a theocratic nation at Mt. Sinai in Holy Scripture has reverberating effects reaching to the culmination of human history. Such insights are indiscernible by the secular historian who may indeed be watching and recording merely political movements on the stage of history.

The writers of Scripture were penmen for God carried along by the Holy Spiritl (II Peter 1:19-21). The "carrying along" elevated their writings into the higher realm of truth unmixed with error. At the same time that carrying along did not obliterate their personalities or native capabilities. Rather it enhanced them.

Our noted American theologian, Carl F.H. Henry, defined the function of the inspiration of the Holy Scriptures.

"Inspiration is that supernatural influence of the Holy Spirit whereby the sacred writers were divinely supervised in their production of Scripture, being restrained from error and guided in the choice of words they used, consistently with their disparate personalities and stylistic peculiarities. God is the source of Holy Scripture; Christ Jesus is the central message; and the Holy Spirit, who inspired it and illumines its message to the reader, bears witness by this inscripturated Word to the Word enfleshed, crucified, risen and returning." *The Expositor's Bible Commentary*, Volume 1, Page 25.

We must rightly affirm, therefore, that the Holy Bible is unique in its own class. We do not classify it among the writings of the ancients, religious or secular. Neither do we relegate it to be the Hebraic and/or Grecian view of philosophy of the cosmos and the history of mankind during the centuries of its composition.

Our confirmation is bounded by our basic premise. The Bible, we contend, is the revelation of God given to men through the instrumentality of chosen men in the past. While the Bible was forged in a historical setting, it is more than history. And while the Bible concentrates on one people, the Israelites, its message is universal because it is the account of God's search for man, first demonstrated in the Garden of Eden when God called to Adam, "Where art thou?" That search for man over the centuries involved the very nature of God, His unqualified holiness.

His unqualified holiness permeates all His divine attributes. Consequently, being unqualifiedly holy He exercises unsullied justice. His unsullied justice provides the basis for His undistorted grace leading to the possibility of His undeserved forgiveness of the penitent. Surely, the all-holy God was under no external compulsion to seek the man whom He had made in His own image and likeness. Instead He was moved by His love to prepare the way for reconciliation with man.

The probation placed before Adam and Eve in the garden was sufficiently clear that no responsibility for its infraction by them could be laid upon their Creator. They were individually responsible and solely answerable to God. Eve's decision to listen to the serpent and eat of the forbidden fruit and Adam's subsequent partaking of it with her opened the ethical sluiceway through which has poured all manner of deviant and diabolic human conduct carrying mankind farther and farther away from the original ethical purity in which the first couple were created. In His perfect foreknowledge and unqualified holiness God saw that creature man's imagination was only evil continually. Hope lay only in some act from His side.

Therefore, in pronouncing the inevitable justice upon the serpent God said, "I will put enmity between . . . thy seed and her seed" (Genesis 3:15).

In these words are found the germinal reason for the revelation of God, the Holy Bible. This Book is the record of God's holy plan to redeem man and God's very good world by His own personal direct involvement. It can not be more concisely or profoundly stated than by the golden text of the Bible, John 3:16. "For God so loved the world that he gave his only begotten son that whosoever believeth on him should not perish but have everlasting life."

Yet, now as then, man seeks to go his own way. But the impossibility of climbing out of the pit he has dug for himself becomes visibly evident by the hundreds of man-made religions in the thousands of people-groups all over the world. Traditional tribal religions cry out for a word from the unknown God. He has spoken but they cannot hear Him because of the cunning craftiness of the serpent still slithering among the trees in every culture. We have the message the people of the world need and are crying for.

Our Bible begins with the announcement of the Seed of the woman and ends with the coronation of the King of kings and Lord of lords. Between these two great mountain peaks lies the plain of the history of man and God's plan of reconciliation through His Anointed, the Messiah, called Christ.

But supposing the Bible is a book produced out of the culture of the ancients, composed or compiled by fallible men, albeit pious men, how can modern man find an authentic word from the God whom he instinctively knows exists?

In recent months attention has once again been given to the origin of the Holy Scriptures. So-called scholars have raised the question, "Who wrote the Bible?" It is not a new question. Doubts have been expressed about the Bible since the days of Eden.

One can quite readily understand why Satan would cast doubt upon God's Word. In order to gain his desired goal to take God's place he must discredit God's Word and if possible lead the assailable to discard the plain Word of God and listen to Satan's word.

Believing as we should that the Bible is God's Holy

Word, we must confidently affirm that when the writers wrote they wrote without error. We readily admit that the autographs were true as they came from the hands of the writers, whether Moses, David, the prophets or the apostles. Those autographs contained no error of fact whether dealing with the origin and consummation of the cosmos or with the relation of the Creator to His universe or with salvation history. The fact that the autographs are lost in no way undermines our basic thesis.

If we concede that the writers were subject to error while writing the Holy Scriptures we are left with an unresolved dilemma, an impossible predicament. There can be no reasonable purpose to search for truth in a Book which contains scraps of truth hidden in the maze of language impounded in error. Such a search will be fruitless.

In contrast we submit not only were the autographs without error but that the transmission of the text of the Holy Bible was preserved by the action of the same Holy Spirit who inspired the writers. We agree with Gleason Archer. We quote from page 86 from the book *The Foundation of Biblical Authority*. "Since the Bible repeatedly affirms that it sets forth the revealed Word of God ('Thus saith the Lord'), rather than the mere conjectures or traditions of men, it must have been preserved in a sufficiently accurate form to achieve its salvific purpose for the benefit of the human race. God is present in Scripture as the omnipotent Lord of history, and as such he could not have allowed his redemptive plan to be thwarted by a seriously defective transmission." We say amen to that!

Self-styled scholars have turned to the Gospels now with their faith-destroying questions. in examining the Gospel of Mark and the recorded sayings of Jesus found in that Gospel, their "scholarly research" has concluded that of the 111 alleged sayings of Jesus found in Mark's Gospel only 17 can be truly ascribed to Him. The rest, they say, are words put in His mouth for preaching values for the apostles and the early church.

Considering that these attacks upon God's Holy Word come from within nominal Christianity, in fact from professors in seminaries and pastors of churches, we conclude the words of Paul are being fulfilled: "For the time will come when they will not endure sound doctrine, but after their own lusts shall heap to themselves teachers having itching ears and they shall turn away their ears from the truth and shall be turned unto fables" (II Timothy 4:3,4).

To these words should be added the words of Peter in II Peter 2:1-3. "But there were false prophets also among the people, even as there shall be false teachers among you, who privily shall bring in damnable heresies, even denying the Lord that bought them and bring upon themselves swift destruction. And many shall follow their pernicious ways; by reason of whom the way of truth shall be evil spoken of. And through covetousness shall they with feigned words make merchandise of you: whose judgment now of a long time lingereth not, and their damnation slumbereth not."

These words follow immediately Peter's great affirmation of the "more sure word of prophecy" in II Peter 1:19-21. When such conditions obtain among the leaders we can expect a powerless church. Under these conditions the people will be seized with such pervasive apathy that the needs of the world will not arouse them.

Beloved, I call to us in the words of the Prophet Hosea in chapter 10, verse 12, "Sow to yourselves in righteousness, reap in mercy; break up your fallow ground: for it is time to seek the LORD till he come and rain righteousness upon you."

Having laid the foundation for a Book of Truth, we

now will seek to show how the divine plan for man's redemption through God's anointed pervades the Holy Bible. I propose to do this in seven unfailing certainties.

I.   CRUSHING THE SERPENT'S HEAD
II.   COMING IN THE FLESH
III. EXPIATING MAN'S SIN
IV.   INTERCEDING MAN'S FAILURE
V.   BLESSING ALL FAMILIES
VI.   OCCUPYING THE PREEMINENCE
VII. REIGNING ON DAVID'S THRONE

I. Crushing the Serpent's Head

This prophecy comes from the mouth of the God of the universe as recorded in Genesis 3:15. "And I will put enmity between thee and the woman, and between thy seed and her seed; it shall bruise thy head, and thou shalt bruise his heel." We should note carefully that the pronoun in "it shall bruise thy head" is a masculine pronoun, he shall bruise thy head. It could be even more dramatic than that. He shall crush thy head. We learn, however, of Eve's sad miscalculation at the birth of Cain, "I have gotten a man from the LORD." She nonetheless speaks of her faith that one would come who hopefully would undo everything that had transpired. But the other half of that prediction is prominently evident first by the murder of Abel by Cain, the man she thought she had from the Lord. Man's cruelty to man appears in the first page of human history. The violence and debasing of all the world in Noah's day tells how successful Satan was in bruising the heel.

Centuries later Pharaoh's decree regarding Israel's boy babies to be cast into the Nile River reveals the demonic plans. So also does Haman's plot to kill all the Jews in Persia in the days of Ahasuerus. The crucifixion of Jesus was Satan's gleeful moment but was blown to bits by the resurrection. This century witnessed the most devastating genocidal attempt in the Nazi's final solution to wipe out the Jews. We understand another attempt to eradicate the Jews will be made by the seven-headed dragon of Revelation 12.

But God does not work by the devil's agenda. Praise the Lord! The time has already been determined by the Amighty when the seed of the woman will crush the serpent's head. Amen.

II. Coming in the Flesh

Here we are faced with the phenomenon beyond human reason. The biblical record teaches us that the first human, Adam, was created in the image and likeness of God. However the second Adam was *God in* human flesh. And so it must be if the Seed of the woman is to crush the serpent's head. The mystery of God in the flesh is not answered by reason but is answered by revelation. Glimpses of this truth are found in such Scriptures as Psalm 2:7, "Thou art my Son; this day have I begotten thee," and in Isaiah 7:14 "Behold, a virgin shall conceive and bear a son, and shall call his name Immanuel."

Several observations must be drawn from Isaiah. First, the word virgin, almah, is always used to designate a chaste virgin and is not the common word for young woman. Second, the word virgin in our Hebrew Bible has a definite article and should be translated *the* virgin. Herein we need to see that the virgin who bore Immanuel was selected by the all-knowing God, else the Scripture would not read *the* virgin.

With this Micah's prophecy is in perfect harmony. "But thou, Bethlehem Ephratah, though thou be little among the thousands of Judah, yet out of thee shall he come forth unto me that is to be ruler in Israel; whose goings forth have been from of old, from everlasting" (Micah 5:2).

Surely there can be no honest question that the One predicted as the eternal One was to come from Bethlehem Ephratah. But centuries passed before the virgin of Nazareth was told she was to bear a Son called "the Son of the Highest."

Modern skeptics reflect the question raised in the hometown of Jesus. His fellow citizens of Nazareth asked, "Is not this Joseph's son?" (Luke 4:22). So the virgin birth is approached from a natural frame. Critics ask the question, "Did Matthew and Luke intend to make a scientific statement?"

The basic underlying question is, "Are miracles possible? Must all phenomena be answered with a natural explanation?" Such questions denigrate the reality of God and His interaction with mankind.

We cannot remove the mystery from the reality of God in the flesh for every miracle has an inexplicable aspect in it. Our human understanding is bound by repeatable phenomena. A miracle is a one-time event. It cannot be repeated for in its uniqueness it defies repetition.

In this miraculous fact of God in flesh lies the magnitude of divine grace. That the One sinned against would die to provide the possibility of pardon for the sinner is surely a demonstration of love far beyond human idealism.

God in flesh was a necessity and became a reality in the purpose and plan of God well stated by Paul in Galatians 4:4,5: "But when the fulness of the time was come, God sent forth his Son, made of a woman, made under the law, To redeem them that were under the law, that we might receive the adoption of sons." Praise God!

III. Expiating Man's Sin

The tragedy of Eden may be seen in a somewhat symbolic way. Adam heard "the voice of the LORD God walking in the garden in the cool of the day." Nightfall was approaching. Day was passing. Indeed the darkness of the separation from God was menacingly near. The result was that the man and his wife were driven out of the Garden, their place of communion with God! Cherubim with a flaming sword stood guard to prohibit another infraction to eat of the tree of life. What they had done once they most likely would do again. So they were driven out and the darkness of the separation from God became a reality.

But the sin of Eve and Adam resulting in their inadequate covering for their nakedness required an act of God. They needed to be covered. So life was given for life. The sentence was ". . . in the day that thou eatest thereof thou shalt surely die" (Genesis 2:17). So God prepared coats of skin to cover them, a stay of death by death. By this act of God in Eden He taught that without blood there is no covering for sin, no remission.

There are clear evidences in the Bible that life for life is the principle by which the unqualifiedly holy God provides for expiation. One deeply emotional example is Abraham offering Isaac. The act was so nearly done that Abraham trusted Jehovah would raise Isaac from the dead in order to keep his covenant with the patriarch. Instead a ram caught in the thicket was the substitutionary sacrifice which saved the son Isaac (Genesis 22). (It should be pointed out that Mt. Moriah and Mt. Calvary are a part of the same mountain. At the one end Abraham offered his son and at the other end God offered His son.)

Another graphic demonstration of substitution and blood is seen in the passover lamb at the time of the exodus of the children of Israel from Egypt. The lamb was to be without blemish. It was to be slain and the blood caught in a basin and applied by hyssop to the doorposts and lintels of the houses to deliver the firstborn son from sure death (Exodus 12). Again it was life for life!

The day of Atonement (Leviticus 16), further indelibly shows how life for life is God's principle for expiation. There were two goats selected. The goat upon which the Lord's lot fell was offered and the blood sprinkled upon the mercy seat. The other goat, called the scapegoat, was released into the wilderness after Aaron had laid his hands upon him and confessed all the iniquities of the people. It was the experience of atoning by blood and the removal of sin to relieve the consequences.

Writers of Old Testament and New Testament books reveal the magnitude of God's plan of expiation. In Isaiah 53 the prophet gives us a dramatic fore gleam of the substitution. Identified as "my servant" in Isaiah 52:13, He is then in chapter 53 further revealed to be the One for the many. Having no sin of His own, He was wounded for us. Life for life is the principle.

All fore gleams focused upon the cross reared on Calvary, outside the city wall. The jeers of the chief priests, scribes and elders were right. "He saved others; himself he cannot save," (Matthew 27:42a).

From Romans 3:19-31 we learn the divine lesson that no sin was truly expiated until Jesus died on the cross and shed His blood. The law brings only the knowledge of sin. The cross brings the expiation of sin. We are freely, without cost, justified by the grace of God through the redemption wrought in Christ Jesus, "Whom God hath set forth to be a propitiation through faith in his blood, to declare his righteousness for the remission of sins that are past, through the forbearance of Godl" (Romans 3:25). Thus sins of the past, present and future to be expiated must have applied the shed blood of God's own Son, the anointed One.

"If we confess our sins, he is faithful and just to forgive us our sins, and to cleanse us from all unrighteousness" (I John 1:9). Amen.

IV. Interceding Man's Failure

No doubt Moses stands head and shoulders above the crowd as a leader. His close association with God is a challenge to us all. In his final addresses to Israel on the plains of Moab he predicted that God would raise up a prophet like him from among Israel's brethren. They were to hear him. Therefore the prophetic ministry of Jesus is early on revealed.

There's another likeness to Moses which the One to be raised would reflect. It is his intercession. In less than three months from the miracles of the Passover and the crossing of the Red Sea Israel fell into idolatry and lusting. Had they lived too long in Egypt?

God took note of their breach of covenant and threatened to destroy them. He offered to make a great nation of Moses. But Moses declined. Moses' intercession for Israel is a type of Jesus' prayer in Gethsemane. Moses pled with God to remember His "covenant with Abraham, Isaac and Jacob." He went so far as to offer himself. He acknowledged the great sin of Israel in making gods of gold right in the shadow of the mountain where the living God had revealed His majesty. Then Moses pled, "Yet now if thou wilt forgive their sin--- ; and if not, blot me, I pray thee, out of thy book which thou hast written (Exodus 32:32).

There was another, Jesus, who prayed with the agony of blood. He said, "Father, if thou be willing, remove this cup from me: nevertheless not my will, but thine, be done" (Luke 22:42). Surely there is no greater commitment than this.

There are indicators in the writings of David which reveal the fact of the priesthood of Jesus. In Psalm 110:4 David by the Spirit predicted, "The LORD hath sworn, and will not repent, Thou art a priest for ever after the order of Melchizedek." Melchizedek was a priest of El Elyon as learned from Genesis 14, but he was not in the priestly line from Abraham! His priestly function was confined to his own personal role.

The book of Hebrews makes a direct connection of Jesus to the priestly order of Melchizedek. While commenting on the call of Aaron to the priesthood as being an office not to be sought after the writer of Hebrews remarks about Christ that He, too, did not glorify Himself. The One who declared the Lord's sonship also said, ". . . Thou art a priest for ever after the order of Melchizedek" (Hebrews 5:61).

This order is clarified in Hebrews 7. Melchizedek had no ancestry or descendants in the priesthood. So Jesus had no priestly line. He was from the tribe of Judah, ". . . of which tribe Moses spake nothing concerning priesthood" (Hebrews 7:14).

Further, by His resurrection He now lives to have an unchanging priesthood. The law could not replace the high priest during his lifetime! Jesus is now alive forevermore and therefore He has an eternal, unchanging priesthood. Now, He having "by Himself purged our sins, sat down on the right hand of the Majesty on high" (Hebrews 1:3b).

We may glory in God's wonderful provision as Paul explains in Romans 8:31-34. "What shall we then say to these things? If God be for us, who can be against us? He that spared not his own Son, but delivered him up for us all, how shall he not with him also freely give us all things? Who shall lay any thing to the charge of God's elect? It is God that justifieth. Who is he that condemneth? It is Christ that died, yea rather, that is risen again, who is even at the right hand of God, who also maketh intercession for us."

And we learn that "there is one God, and one mediator between God and men, the man Christ Jesus" (I Timothy 2:5). Amen.

V. Blessing All Families

The Patriarch Abraham was called to stand under the cloudless mideast sky and hear God say, "Look now toward heaven, and tell the stars, if thou be able to number them, so shall thy seed be" (Genesis 15:5).

Abraham's initial call from Ur of the Chaldeas included a specific reference to a blessing for all families of the earth (Genesis 12:3). But Abraham's patience was running out. His complaint to God in Genesis 15 that Eliezer of Damascus would be his heir was the occasion of God's challenge to Abraham to count the stars. The Scripture tells us that Abraham believed God and it was counted to him for righteousness (Genesis 15:6).

Yet, Abraham's patience was exhausted. So when Sarai offered him her Egyptian maid to bear him a son he yielded believing when Ishmael was born that his seed had been secured. However, Abraham's way was not God's way. When Ishmael was 12 years old God assured Abraham and Sarah they would have a son. Furthermore, God named him. He called him Isaac.

The test came to Abraham, however, after his son Isaac was a youth. God tested him and called him to offer his son as a burnt offering. Three lonely days passed as they made their way toward Mt. Moriah. There Abraham carried out the command until the angel of the LORD arrested him and said, "Lay not thine hand upon the lad, neither do thou any thing unto him: for now I know that thou fearest God, seeing thou has not withheld thy son, thine only son from me " (Genesis 22:12).

Then after the offering of the ram in Isaac's place, the angel of the LORD spoke again to Abraham and said, "By myself have I sworn, saith the LORD, for because thou hast done this thing, and hast not withheld thy son, thine only son: That in blessing I will bless thee, and in multiplying I will multiply thy seed as the stars of the heaven, and as the sand which is upon the sea shore; and thy seed shall possess the gate of his enemies; And in thy seed shall all the nations of the earth be blessed; because thou hast obeyed my voice" (Genesis 22:16-18). Clearly then the seed of Abraham was to be a blessing to all families of the earth.

When we begin reading the Gospel of Matthew we learn that the genealogy of Jesus begins like this: "The book of the generation of Jesus Christ, the son of David, the son of Abraham" (Matthew 1:1).

Turning then to the interpretation of the Apostle Paul for the meaning of seed, we learn that Paul defined the seed as one, not many. He wrote like this: "Now to Abraham and his seed were the promises made. He saith not, And to seeds, as of many; but as of one, And to thy seed, which is Christ" (Galatians 3:16). And then he goes on, "And this I say, that the covenant, that was confirmed before of God in Christ, the law, which was four hundred and thirty years after, cannot disannul, that it should make the promise of none effect. For if the inheritance be of the law, it is no more of promise: but God gave it to Abraham by promise" (Galatians 3:16-18).

The universal scope of all families is clarified by the Apostle Paul in Galatians 3 further. "For ye are all the children of God by faith in Christ Jesus. For as many of you as have been baptized into Christ have put on Christ. There is neither Jew nor Greek, there is neither bond nor free, there is neither male nor female: for ye are all one in Christ

Jesus. And if ye be Christ's, then are ye Abraham's seed, and heirs according to the promise" (Galatians 3:26-29).

Paul further elaborated on the universal blessing of Christ as he writes to the Romans. "That if thou shalt confess with thy mouth the Lord Jesus, and shalt believe in thine heart that God hath raised him from the dead, thou shalt be saved. For with the heart man believeth unto righteousness; and with the mouth confession is made unto salvation. For the Scripture saith, Whosoever believeth on him shall not be ashamed. For there is no difference between the Jew and the Greek: for the same Lord over all is rich unto all that call upon him. For whosoever shall call upon the name of the Lord shall be saved" (Romans 10:9-13).

John, the Seer on Patmos, witnessed the testimony of the twenty-four elders before the throne of God. He wrote: "And when he had taken the book, the four beasts and four and twenty elders fell down before the Lamb, having every one of them harps, and the golden vials full of odours, which are the prayers of saints. And they sang a new song, saying Thou are worthy to take the book, and to open the seals thereof: for thou wast slain, and hast redeemed us to God by, thy blood out of every kindred, and tongue and people and nation; And hast made us unto our God kings and priests: and we shall reign on the earth" (Revelation 5:8-10). Yes, praise God! The blessing is to all nations.

And there is another reference to be mentioned. A great multitude stood before the throne of God as John reported it, "After this I beheld, and, lo, a great multitude, which no man could number, of all nations, and kindreds, and people, and tongues, stood before the throne, and before the Lamb, clothed with white robes, and palms in their hands; And cried with a loud voice, saying Salvation to our God which sitteth upon the throne, and unto the Lamb" (Revelation 7:9,10).

From the question one of the elders asked John, who turned it back to the questioner, he learned, "And I said unto him, Sir, thou knowest. And he said to me, These are they which came out of great tribulation, and have washed their robes, and made them white in the blood of the Lamb" (Revelation 7:14).

We must not overlook the fact that the word tribulation has a definite article in the Greek New Testament. Thus we understand the tribulation referred to is the great one, about to be released as the judgment of God upon rebellious mankind. But out of the tribulation, that is the great one, an innumerable multitude will be gathered from all nations.

The blessing to all nations is released through Jesus, the Anointed One, the seed of Abraham. Yes, Amen.

VI. Occupying the Preeminence

When the LORD God created the first man he was perfect in all aspects, body, soul and spirit, since he was in the image and likeness of God, his Creator. The sin of Eden defaced that image and likeness so that since the sin of Eden, man has been less than perfect. In all his striving of whatever nature, he has always fallen short of the ideal expressed by the LORD God. "Be ye holy for I am holy."

If there was ever to be a restoration of Edenic conditions then another perfect man needed to come on the human scene. Such a Man is the Son of Mary, the virgin of Nazareth.

As we have shown, the virgin birth was necessary to break the transmission of Adamic depravity to the offspring. Therefore, we affirm that Jesus' human nature was like Adam's before he sinned–perfect, not depraved. Furthermore, according to Jesus' own words He always pleased the Father, even to His death on the cross.

At His baptism, the voice from heaven confirmed the true role Jesus was to fill. Accompanying the descent of the Holy Spirit the Voice said, "This is my beloved Son, in whom I am well pleased," (Matthew 3:17). So at the beginning of His ministry Jesus had the testimony of the Father that He had a unique place to fill.

Near the close of His ministry, with Peter, James and John to witness, He was transfigured, metamorphosed, with a countenance radiant as the sun and garments white as the light. Out of the overshadowing shekinah glory cloud the Voice spoke, "This is my beloved Son in whom I am well pleased; hear ye him" (Matthew 17:5b).

The Gospels bear record of His single uniqueness. Temple guards testified, "Never man spake like this man" (John 7:46).

When the crowds became hostile He passed through their midst and no one laid hands on Him. But the time came when He yielded Himself to them. And they bound Him and led Him away even though He told Peter He could have called twelve legions of angels and been delivered.

At the time it appeared to the disciples and to the opposition that the cross and the tomb ended His career. If death ended it for others, they thought it ended it for Him, too. However, they did not consider the insight Peter expressed in his sermon on Pentecost. Peter addressed the men of Israel pointing out that death could not possibly hold Jesus. His life was approved of God and was without sin. For that basic reason death had no holding power on His body.

Adam suffered death because he sinned. Jesus never sinned so death was powerless to hold Him. His resurrection then must be the basis upon which His preeminence rests.

In developing his argument further on Pentecost Peter

quoted Psalm 110:1: "The LORD said unto my Lord, Sit thou at my right hand, until I make thine enemies thy footstool." So Jesus Christ has been exalted to be both Lord, kurios, and Christ, the anointed one.

To this David also agreed in Psalm 2. "Ask of me, and I shall give thee the heathen for thine inheritance, and the uttermost parts of the earth for thy possession. Thou shalt break them with a rod of iron; thou shalt dash them in pieces like a potter's vessel. Be wise, now therefore, O ye kings: be instructed, ye judges of the earth. Serve the LORD with fear, and rejoice with trembling"(Psalm 2:8-11).

In his opening words to the Romans, Paul set forth our Christian promise regarding the preeminence of Jesus. "Concerning his Son Jesus Christ our Lord, which was made of the seed of David according to the flesh; And declared to be the Son of God with power, according to the spirit of holiness, by the resurrection from the dead: By whom we have received grace and apostleship for obedience to the faith among all nations, for his name" (Romans 1:3-5).

Probably the loftiest text is found in Colossians 1:9-18. Paul's desire was that the Colossian believers might be filled with the knowledge of his will in all wisdom and spiritual understanding. He wished for them to experience the deliverance from the power of darkness and to be translated into the kingdom of God's dear Son being redeemed through his blood.

Verses 15-18 are of the highest eloquence. "Who is the image of the invisible God, the firstborn of every creature: For by him were all things created, that are in heaven, and that are in earth, visible and invisible, whether they be thrones, or dominions, or principalities, or powers: all things were created by him, and for him. And he is before all things, and by him all things consist. And he is the head of the body, the church: who is the beginning, the firstborn from the dead; that in all things he might have the preeminence" (Colossians 1:15-18).

Here we see that He is the image of the invisible God, the first of all creatures and Creator of all things in heaven, in earth, the visible and invisible. Not only did He create all things, but by Him all things consist, that is, are held together. He is the head of the church, the beginning, the firstborn of the dead, that in all He might have the preeminence, meaning no one is above Him.

Preeminence means every knee will bow and every tongue will confess that He is Lord to the glory of God the Father (Philippians 2:10,11).

We rightly call Him *LORD*, by which is meant He holds the position of absolute preeminence. Amen.

VII. Reigning on David's Throne

The implication of this concept is far-reaching. Surely the dominion right bestowed on the first Adam, which he lost due to his sin in Eden, we should expect to see bestowed on the second Adam. We may rightly say what Adam lost by his sin in the Garden of Eden, Jesus won by His submission in the Garden of Gethsemane. The right of dominion entailed the responsibility of obedience to the LORD of all.

From Jesus' earthly life certain teachers see Him as the weak, ineffective rabble rouser. He fouled up with the leaders of His time. His teaching, they say, aroused the ire of the establishment to the fever point of collaboration to bring Him to death by Roman decree to be crucified.

It is true. At the time of His death the hecklers were there to challenge Him with, "If he be the King of Israel let him now come down from the cross and we will believe him" (Matthew 27:42). Others taunted Him, "If thou be the Son of God come down from the cross" (Matthew 27:40). What they and even His disciples failed to understand was the dual ministry which He had to perform. He was to be first the perfect sacrifice for sin, and second the ruling monarch to whom every knee will bow and whose Lordship every tongue will confess. He could not be the Lord or the King before He became the Saviour. Therefore, nothing was postponed. Everything was carried out according to the divine plan during His earthly ministry including His resurrection and ascension to glory to be seated at the right hand of God until the appointed time.

"The LORD said unto my Lord sit thou on my right hand until I make thine enemies thy footstool" (Psalm 110:1). Two particulars must be observed in these words. First, it is a clear statement by the LORD Jehovah to the Lord, Adonai. Second, a period of time is defined with a change indicated by the word "until." Therefore, the place at the right hand is only for a period of time. Its length is stated as being until the enemies are subdued.

The dominion status given to the perfect second Adam has its roots in the line of David, already stated to David near the end of his life. Nathan, the prophet, turned David's desire to build a house for God into a declaration that God would build a house for David by establishing his throne forever. David would never lack a man to sit upon his throne.

While the concept was overwhelming to David yet in his prayer of acceptance he said, "And now, O Lord GOD, thou art that God, and thy words be true, and thou hast promised this goodness unto thy servant: Therefore now let it please thee to bless the house of thy servant, that it may continue for ever before thee: for thou, O Lord GOD, hast spoken it: and with thy blessing let the house of thy servant be blessed for ever."

But to have an everlasting throne, there needs to be

an everlasting person. That person unmistakably is Jesus of Nazarth, born of the virgin and legal Son of Joseph, who has risen from the dead.

In his announcement to Mary the angel Gabriel clearly stated, "And behold, thou shalt conceive in thy womb, and bring forth a son, and shalt call his name JESUS. He shall be great, and shall be called the Son of the Highest: and the Lord God shall give unto him the throne of his father David: And he shall reign over the house of Jacob for ever; and of his kingdom there shall be no end" (Luke 1:31-3).

To Mary this could only mean that her Son was to be the ruler on David's throne. Amen. How the full extent of Gabriel's prophecy would be fulfilled she did not know but she willingly said, "Behold the handmaid of the Lord; be it unto me according to thy word . . ." (Luke 1:38). By her yieldedness the purpose and plan of God was carried forward.

But now how will the risen Ruler take His rightfully designated place? Critics have assailed the concept from various angles. They have emptied the prophecy to mean a merely spiritual kingdom by misunderstanding certain isolated texts such as Luke 17:20,21. "And when he was demanded of the Pharisees, when the kingdom of God should come, he answered them and said, The kingdom of God cometh not with observation: Neither shall they say, Lo here! or, lo there! for, behold, the kingdom of God is within you."

The idea of "within you" can better be expressed by the phrase "among you." The kingdom of God is among you, certainly not within the hearts and lives of those hypocritical Pharisees to whom He was addressing His word.

And Romans 14:17 states, "For the kingdom of God is not meat and drink; but righteousness, and peace, and joy in the Holy Ghost." Indeed, the kingdom of God is not meat and drink. It will be righteousness of the highest order.

The critics also have overlooked the full teaching of I Corinthians 15:50. "Now this I say, brethren, that flesh and blood cannot inherit the kingdom of God; neither doth corruption inherit incorruption." This text makes it abundantly clear that the kingdom of God is a post resurrection kingdom, for flesh and blood is a present condition. Corruption cannot inherit the kingdom of God. It must be incorruption.

Certainly, the right hand of God cannot be the location of the throne of David. There is only one proper place for David's throne. It is Jerusalem.

As Jesus taught the disciples to pray, He said, "After this manner therefore pray ye: Our Father who art in heaven, Hallowed be thy name. Thy kingdom come. Thy will be done in earth, as it is in heaven. Give us this day our daily bread. And forgive us our debts as we forgive our debtors. And lead us not into temptation, but deliver us from evil: For thine is the kingdom, and the power, and the glory, forever. Amen" (Matthew 6:9-13).

Careful attention must be given to the petition, "Thy kingdom come." Many, today, take this to be a process initiated and carried on through human effort. If that were the meaning the petition should read, "Help us to bring in thy kingdom."

However the full meaning of the brief petition is, the kingdom will come as an *event* not as a *process* which a careful interpretation will reveal. The kingdom, therefore, will come when the King comes back. Jesus' parable of the nobleman going to receive a kingdom in Luke 19:11-27 is a clear example of this. The introductory phrase there is that He gave this parable because He was near Jerusalem and because some people thought that the kingdom of God should immediately appear.

It must be remembered that the citizens of a kingdom have nothing to do with choosing the king or defining the kingdom. That is only the right of the One bestowing, the One who has the authority. Therefore, Christians today are not "kingdom builders."

In the commission Jesus gave the disciples, He said nothing at all about their responsibility to bring in the kingdom. Rather they were to go and make disciples of all nations. They were to be witnesses unto Him unto the uttermost parts of the world.

For the true picture of the King in His rightful role we turn to Revelation 19 where the Seer on Patmos saw Him coming crowned with many crowns to rule the nations with a rod of iron and tread the winepress of the wrath of Almighty God. His first act will be to smite the armies of the beast and the false prophet with the sword of His mouth and to consign the beast and false prophet to the lake of fire. See Revelation 19:11-21. So at last the perfect Man, the descendant of David crowned with many crowns will occupy David's throne as a forever king! Amen.

Then will come to pass the prophecy given to the disciples when Peter asked what they shall have because they have forsaken all and followed Jesus. "And Jesus said unto them, Verily I say unto you, that ye which have followed me, in the regeneration when the Son of man shall sit on the throne of his glory, ye also shall sit upon twelve thrones, judging the twelve tribes of Israel" (Matthew 19:28). Amen.

From this study we, therefore, conclude the Bible is foremost the revelation from God to man tracing the plan of God for the redemption of man through the gift and ministry of the Son of God. He is the perfect man. He is God in the flesh who will complete the plan of God to bring in the new heavens and the new earth wherein dwells righteousness. The Bible is God's Book detailing history from eternity to eternity. Its words are directed to earth-dwellers in the time frame of mortality.

Jesus, the incarnate God-man, will fulfill all that has been spoken about Him. To Him be all the glory, world without end. Amen!

J. Otis Yoder is President, Heralds of Hope Radio Ministry, Breezewood, PA.

Presented at the Annual Conference of The Fellowship of Concerned Mennonites, October 4-6, 1991, at Pleasant View Mennonite Church, Hutchinson, Kansas.

FIVE

Passing the Torch of Truth

by George R. Brunk II

THE SUBJECT IN FOCUS here is the passing of the truth, not only from one generation to another, but from those who possess the truth to those who possess it not. Simply put, it is a matter of communicating the truth to others, whether they be in our own families, neighbors, friends, people at home or abroad. It is a question of compliance with the mandate of the great commission.

William Temple once said, "The fact that you are not passing it on proves that you haven't got it; and if you have got it, it will make you pass it on because of what it is." It has been said that a nonwitnessing follower of Christ is a contradiction in terms.

It is possible for a messenger to run when he has no message, and it is possible for one to have a message but refuse to run. One may well question whether a professed Christian who has no passion for the truth and the salvation of the lost, is indeed a Christian at all. It may be no exaggeration to say that many professed believers are like an automobile salesman who never makes a sale, or a fisherman who never catches fish.

The first and primary opportunity of passing on the truth is in the family. Let us not forget the instruction which

Moses gave to the Children of Israel as recorded in Deuteronomy 6:4-9. The first admonition here is that the one who is to pass on the truth shall "love the Lord thy God with all thy heart, and with all thy soul, and with all thy might. And these words, which I command thee this day, shall be in thine heart; and thou shalt teach them diligently to thy children. . . ." Here the emphasis is upon a living and vital experience of the truth before one is qualified to pass it on, even to his own children. Parents who are superficial and unspiritual are without the qualifications of passing it on to their children. But we must recognize that sometimes the best of parents must suffer the rebellion and unbelief of disobedient children.

The Right and Wrong Ways to Leave the Faith

In the sixth chapter of Hebrews, we are told what is the right and wrong way to leave the faith. The right way to leave it is to build upon it as one builds upon a foundation. The wrong way to leave it is to renounce, deny, or repudiate it. A builder, after laying a solid foundation, then leaves it in the erection of the superstructure. That foundation might never be seen again, but nevertheless is fulfilling its purpose. But, then, "if the foundations be destroyed," what will the people do? Are we not witnessing in our time the breakup and the repudiation of truths that are foundational?

We are warned over and over in the Scriptures of those who have denied the faith (I Tim. 5:7), or have cast off their faith (I Tim. 5:12), or of those who overthrew the faith of some" (I Tim. 2:17). In I Tim. 6:10, Paul refers to those who "have erred [been seduced, Margin] from the faith, and pierced themselves through with many sorrows." In the verses that follow, he says, "O man of God, *flee* these things; and *follow* after righteousness, godliness, faith, love, patience, meekness. *Fight* the good fight of faith and lay hold on eternal life, whereunto thou art also called, and has professed a good profession before many witnesses."

We observe here that the three key words seem to be these: flee, follow, and fight. A similar passage is found in II Timothy 2:22 where the believer is admonished to "*flee* also youthful lusts: but *follow* righteousness, faith, charity, peace, with them that call on the Lord out of a pure heart."

In keeping the faith, it is necessary for one to literally flee from evil. According to these Scriptures, it is also necessary for him to follow. The Apostle Paul was the kind of leader who could admonish believers to follow him as he followed Christ. "For yourselves know how ye ought to follow us; for we behaved not ourselves disorderly among you" (II Thess. 3:7).

Keeping and communicating the truth also involves a fight. The believer is supplied with armor (with weapons) for the downfall of strongholds of Satan. The believer is admonished to war a good warfare. It is a good fight which we are commanded to engage in so that we might "lay hold on eternal life, whereunto thou art also called, and hast professed a good profession before many witnesses."

The great Apostle Paul was able to say, "So fight I, not as one that beateth the air" (I Cor. 9:26). He could say of himself, "I have fought a good fight, I have finished my course, I have kept the faith" (II Tim. 4:7).

It is to be feared that some professed believers have become so confused in their understanding of the doctrine of nonresistance that they have completely lost their ability to fight the powers of darkness or to put on the whole armor of God. How pathetic it is that some believers consume their energies by involvement in internal conflict or fights with other believers! Passing the torch of truth involves an understanding of who the real enemy is and how to resist the powers of darkness. Is it not possible for an individual to fight against those he ought to support, and support causes against which he should fight?

Fighting, like contention, can be good or bad. The right kind of contention is referred to in Jude 3, "Beloved, when I gave all diligence to write unto you of the common salvation, it was needful for me to write unto you and exhort you that ye should earnestly contend for the faith which was once delivered unto the saints."

Moreover, the New Testament model for passing the torch of truth involves holding fast. Paul admonishes the believers to prove all things, hold fast that which is good (I Thess. 5:21) and he appeals to the brethren at Thessalonica to "stand fast and hold the traditions which you have been taught, whether by word, or our epistle" (II Thess. 2:15). Paul also admonishes Timothy to "hold fast the form of sound words which thou hast heard of me" (II Tim. 1:13). This admonition of the Holy Spirit through the Apostle Paul deserves our attention and obedience in this time of such compromise and accommodation.

The writer of the Book of Hebrews makes frequent reference to holding fast–"firm unto the end" (Heb. 3:6); of holding "the beginning of our conscience firm unto the end" (Heb. 3:14); and again "let us hold fast our profession" (Heb. 4:14). In 10:23, believers are admonished to "hold fast the profession of our faith without wavering."

John, the revelator, also makes reference to the importance of holding fast. The Lord of the Church says in Revelation 2:25, "Hold fast till I come" and "Hold fast that which thou hast; let no man take thy crown."

The implication in these passages seems to be that there will be a terrible storm in the end time which will make it necessary for true believers to "take fast hold of instruction," lest they waver or lose their crown.

We have seen in the above passages that there is a right and a wrong way to leave the faith, that it is necessary to flee, to follow, to fight, to contend earnestly for the faith, to prove all things, and to hold fast that which is good, lest one waver and lose his crown.

Are We Passing Our Faith on to Our Youth?

There was an interesting meeting recently of about two dozen evangelical scholars who met in Washington to discuss this question. Their conversation centered around a recent publication by a sociologist at the University of Virginia, James Davison Hunter, who suggests in his book that evangelicals might be properly concerned about the beliefs of their young people. Between 1982-1985 Hunter made a study of such well-known Christian colleges as Wheaton, Gordon, Westmont, Taylor, Messiah, George Fox, Bethel, Seattle Pacific, and Houghton along with leading theological seminaries, Fuller, Gordon-Conwell, Westminster, Ashbury, and Talbot.

The prominent American theologian Carl F. H. Henry made these blunt observations about conditions as he has observed them in his academic career (p. 6, March 11, *World*). "When one focuses not on marginal but on centrally important control-beliefs, the evangelical campuses surveyed, as a group, do reflect disconcerting theological deterioration. Moreover, in my graduate teaching on numerous seminary campuses, I have confirmed to my own satisfaction the accuracy of Hunter's indications for example, that even on some of the best evangelical college campuses some professors have taught their students that Jesus Christ is not the sole ground of human acceptance by God, and that the entire human race need not have descended from Adam."

Henry continued: "Other important theological modifications have wider currency. Not least is the growing acceptance in evangelical seminaries and colleges of a neo-orthodox view of scripture, that accepts biblical teaching as fallible witness at the expense of its comprehensive authority and reliability. Since the dialectical view excludes propositional revelation, and Karl Barth consequently held that the Christian revelation does not involve a given world view, the consequences for revealed doctrine and for evangelical world view exposition are enormous."

Some parents are waking up to the fact that they have not done very well in passing on to their youth the convictions and views which they have held dear. Some parents are testifying that there is a vastly greater difference between them and their children than there is between them and their parents.

One writer says that it may be a shock to the reader, but youth sitting in pews all across America are guzzling, smoking, snorting, dropping and slamming drugs into their bodies. Also, a new survey recently released from the University of Colorado gives some very shocking and enlightening information as to the extent of drug use among young people who are identified with the church. The study involving nearly 14,000 junior high and high school youth showed that the young people of the so-called church are as involved as those who are unchurched. Note these shocking figures. Eighty percent of church young people reported drinking beer as compared to eighty-eight percent of the unchurched youth. Thirty-eight percent of the church young people had tried marijuana while forty-seven percent of the unchurched youth have done so. Fifty-eight percent of the church teens have used tobacco as compared to sixty-five percent of the unchurched. Twenty-two percent of the churched young people had tried barbiturates with twenty-eight percent unchurched doing the same.

One may well ask the question whether the church is affecting the young people as positively as is commonly thought. There is not the difference between the churched and the unchurched that one would expect.

Other studies have showed also that there is only a slight difference in the moral level of the churches' youth and the unchurched. Among both there is a very high percentage of promiscuity and sexual activity.

One may inquire whether the picture is all that negative. Is there nothing to be said of a positive nature about the developments of our time? The answer is yes, of course. One could go on and on to identify positive changes that have taken place over the last fifty years or so. One could refer to the greater participation of the young people in the life of the church, mention could be made of the increased conviction for outreach and missionary activity. There are many more people who are involved in voluntary service. There are more opportunities for young people to secure training and preparation for service in the kingdom of God. There has been notable increase of giving on the part of the Church at large. Some would even argue that the quality of preaching today is superior to that of a generation ago.

It is not easy for us to arrive at a balanced evaluation of our times. It will seem that some are unable to see anything good and others are unable to see anything bad.

In the Oct. 1985 issue of *Eternity* magazine, Joseph Bayly makes this evaluation of the times which is not very optimistic.

> We inherited the integrity of marriage and the family; we bequeath a new permissiveness toward divorce and a new pattern of single-parent families.

We inherited a clearly defined, biblical value system; we bequeath shattered values.

We inherited belief in the humanness of unborn babies and the criminality of murdering them in the uterus. We bequeath an unending American Holocaust of 19 million corpses, increasing at the rate of 1.5 million a year. We also bequeath a general unconcern among evangelical Christians.

We inherited doctrinal, expository preaching with a heavy emphasis on prophecy. We bequeath relational preaching with a heavy emphasis on success here and now.

We inherited leaders who spoke out against evil in society and the church; we bequeath leaders who are specialists in public relations and fundraising.
. . .

We inherited deep distrust of commercial entertainment, typified by sanctions against movie-going. We bequeath acceptance of every kind of entertainment in the living room, available to children. . . .

We inherited homes and churches that were patriarchal, overseas missions that were to a large extent matriarchal. We bequeath an unsolved problem of reconciling the Bible with cultural change in the role of women.

We inherited family togetherness and activities; we bequeath age-level activities and small groups in the church.

We inherited government friendly toward the church and a church uninvolved in government. We bequeath government hostile toward the church and the church enmeshed in politics and civil religion.

George R. Brunk II is editor of the Sword and Trumpet and Executive Director of FCM, Harrisonburg, VA.